BIRD CAGES BY HENDRYX

Retro Peacock Edition, 1938

Introduction by R. Peacock

**THE ANDREW B. HENDRYX CO.,
NEW HAVEN, CONN.**

Chicago Warehouse: 1327 West Washington Boulevard

Published in 2013 by Retro Peacock Books
Toronto, Canada
www.RetroPeacock.com

This book was originally published as an illustrated catalogue in 1938 by The Andrew B. Hendryx Company.

To stay informed about upcoming Retro Peacock editions, please visit www.RetroPeacock.com.

No part of the contents of this publication may be reproduced or used in any form or by any means—graphic, electronic, or mechanical, including photocopying, recording, or information storage-and-retrieval systems—without the written permission of the publisher.

© 2013 Retro Peacock Books
All rights reserved

Printed in the United States of America

First edition

ISBN-13: 978-0986863714
ISBN-10: 0986863718

INTRODUCTION

For many Americans living in the twentieth century, the name "Hendryx" is synonymous with elegant bird cages. With the ubiquity of the Hendryx brand, these bird cages could be seen wherever America's beloved winged songsters were kept as pets. In the present day, the most prized bird cages surviving in American antique shops are of the Hendryx variety – a testament to the timeless success of this company.

The Andrew B. Hendryx Company was established by its namesake in 1869 on Audubon Street in New Haven, Connecticut. By the early 1900s, the company workforce blossomed to over 200 employees from a total of 25 in its initial years. Under the leadership of its founder, the Andrew B. Hendryx Company became a fixture in New Haven, providing an economic stimulus to the surrounding area known at the time as an industrial manufacturing centre. During the first half of the twentieth century, Hendryx bird cages were seen in shops and catalogs all over the United States, and the company became a household name famous for its popular bird cages used to house equally popular songbirds as pets.

By the 1920s, the Andrew B. Hendryx Company had become the largest birdcage manufacturer in the United States. The company advertised nationally in magazines to demonstrate the many benefits of having a pet songbird. One example of this promotion is "The Feathered Philosopher," the story of a pet bird who guides a family of musicians to discover true happiness. This story was contained in a free pamphlet which was given out to customers. Advertisements for the company were woven inconspicuously into the story's illustrations.

By the latter half of the twentieth century, production at the Andrew B. Hendryx manufacturing plant on Audubon Street began to curtail with the decline of the industrial era. The business was eventually sold to another pet supply company, and the last remains of the former manufacturing empire on Audubon Street were sold at an auction in 1996.

Though the remains of the Hendryx factory can no longer be seen in the rejuvenated urban landscape of New Haven, the legacy of Andrew B. Hendryx lives on in every one of the many surviving cages that left the doors of his factory before it was permanently shuttered. With its unparalleled ubiquity, Hendryx will forever be respected and celebrated as "The Great Name in Cages."

– **R. PEACOCK**

RETROPEACOCK.COM

THE "HOUSE OF HENDRYX"

A Record of Achievement

As our New 1938 Catalog No. 46 is being placed in the mails, the 20 Millionth Hendryx Bird Cage leaves the factory assembly lines, and starts on its journey to gladden the life of some little Feathered Songster in another American home.

Twenty Million Hendryx Cages in Twenty Million Homes have made the name HENDRYX a household word wherever Song Birds are treasured as family Pets.

But the glory of past achievement quickly dims in the anticipation of future accomplishments just ahead.

Other Millions of Bird Lovers of the new generation continue to demand HENDRYX Cages to house other Millions of Winsome Warblers.

The New, Modern, Colorful HENDRYX Cages illustrated in this Catalog continue the most salable, the most profitable, the most popular Products of their kind in America today.

The "House of Hendryx" Marches On.

THE ANDREW B. HENDRYX CO.

NEW HAVEN, CONN.,

U. S. A.

Who Am I?

I AM a friend of All, young or old, sick or well, rich or poor.

I CONVERSE with All, in the universal language of Song.

I AM the living symbol of joy and love, singing my way into the hearts of people everywhere.

I AM a silver tongued, winged minstrel. I triumph over gloom.

MY COAT is the color of golden sunshine, my sunrise song an ecstasy of joy.

I AM a feathered philosopher, softening the drab moments of life with the courage of my song.

I AM—
your Pet Canary.

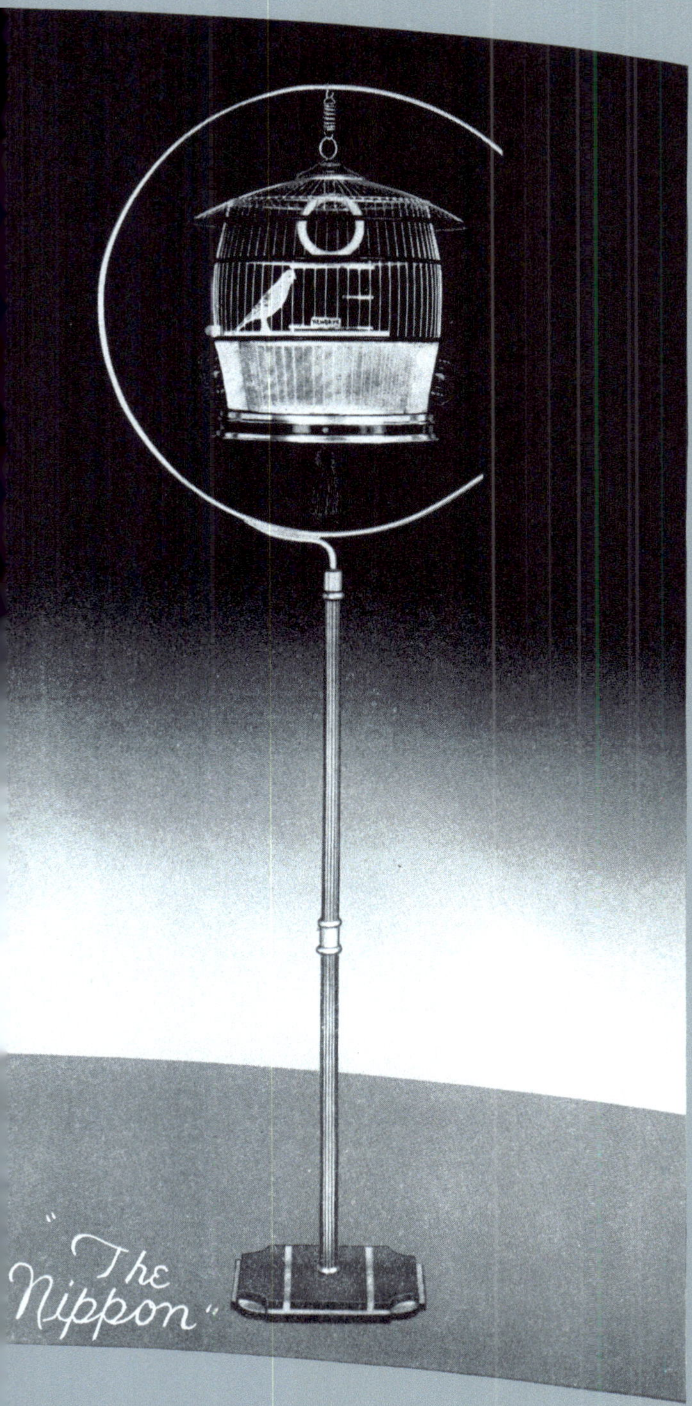

HENDRYX

"The Nippon"

Cage 2075, Stand S700

A beautifully developed Model with Oriental Motif.

SIZE—12¼ in. dia. 16 in. high.
FINISH—Chromium with Black Trim. Brass Construction.
PACKED—1 in Carton. Weight, 12 lbs.

STAND

HEIGHT—5 ft. 8 in. 2 Pc. Upright of 1 in. dia. Fluted Tubing.
FINISH—Lustrous Chromium.
PACKED—1 KD in Carton. Weight, 13 lbs.

"The Palace"

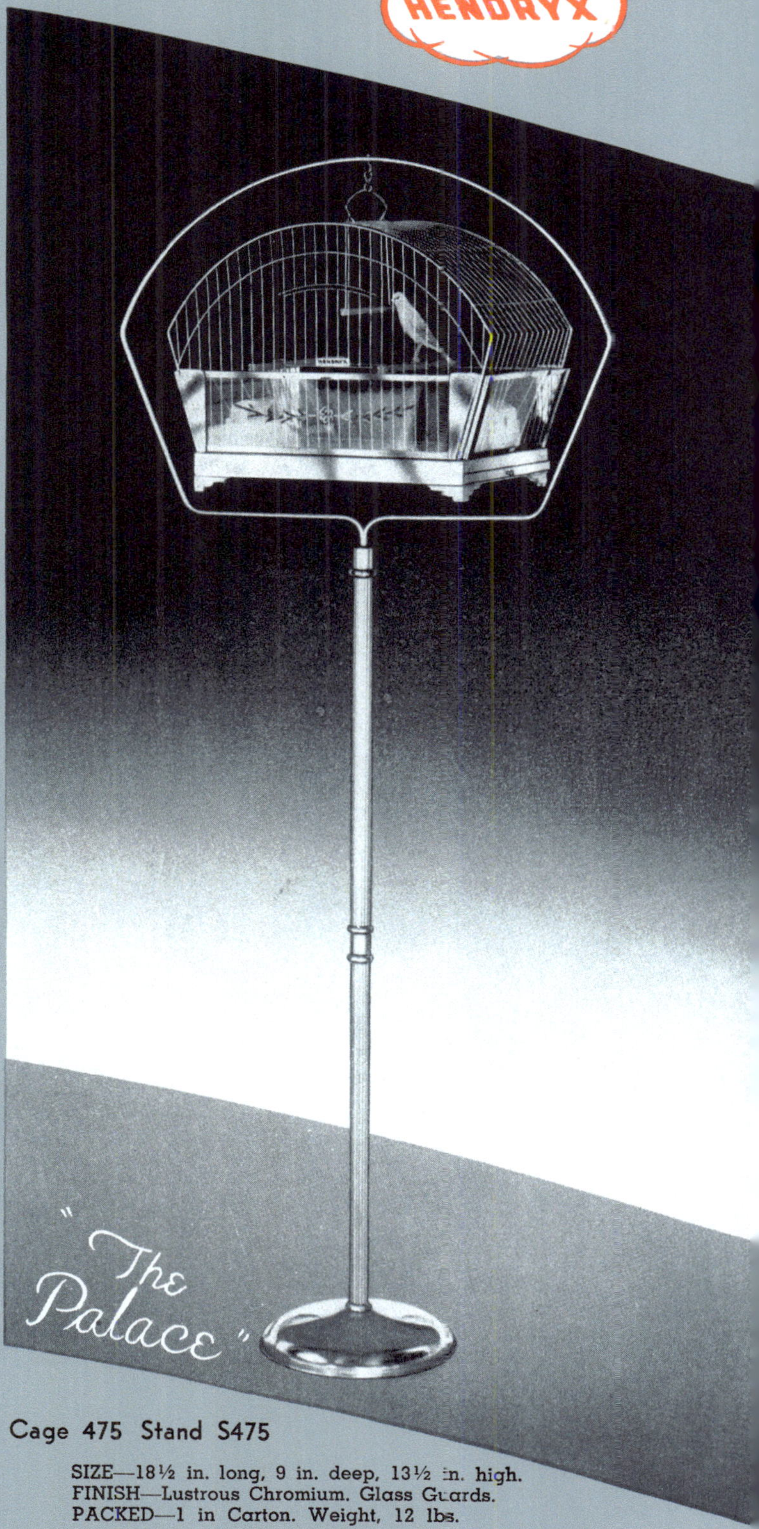

Cage 475 Stand S475

SIZE—18½ in. long, 9 in. deep, 13½ in. high.
FINISH—Lustrous Chromium. Glass Guards.
PACKED—1 in Carton. Weight, 12 lbs.

STAND

HEIGHT—5 ft. 4½ in. 2 Pc. Upright 1 in. dia. Tubing.
FINISH—Lustrous Chromium.
PACKED—1 KD in Carton. Weight, 13 lbs.

hendryx

"The Quad"
Cage 720 Stand S75

SIZE—12½ in. long, 9 in. deep, 15½ in. high.
FINISH—Solid Brass Beautifully Polished and Lacquered.
PACKED—1 in Carton. Weight, 11 lbs.
STAND
HEIGHT—5 ft. 8¾ in. 2 Pc. Fluted Upright.
FINISH—Lacquered Brass.
PACKED—1 KD in Carton. Weight, 13 lbs.

Page Four

"The Duchess"
Cage 2275, Stand S22

A true aristocrat, perfectly proportioned and of never-ending popularity.

SIZE—11 in. dia. 14½ in. high.
FINISH—Solid Brass beautifully Polished and Lacquered.
PACKED—1 in Carton. Weight, 8 lbs.
STAND
HEIGHT—5 ft. 8 in. 2 Pc. Upright of ⅞ in. dia. Tubing.
FINISH—Black Base and Upright, Brass Arch.
PACKED—1 KD in Carton. Weight, 10 lbs.

HENDRYX

"The Pagoda"

Cage JC, Stand SJC

SIZE—11 in. dia. 18 in. high.
FINISH—Lustrous Chromium with Black, Red or Green Trim.
PACKED—1 in Carton. Weight, 7 lbs.

STAND

HEIGHT—5 ft. 5½ in. 2 Pc. Upright ⅞ in. dia. Tubing.
FINISH—Black, Red or Green with Chromium Arch.
PACKED—1 KD in Carton. Weight, 13 lbs.

"The Canarycote"

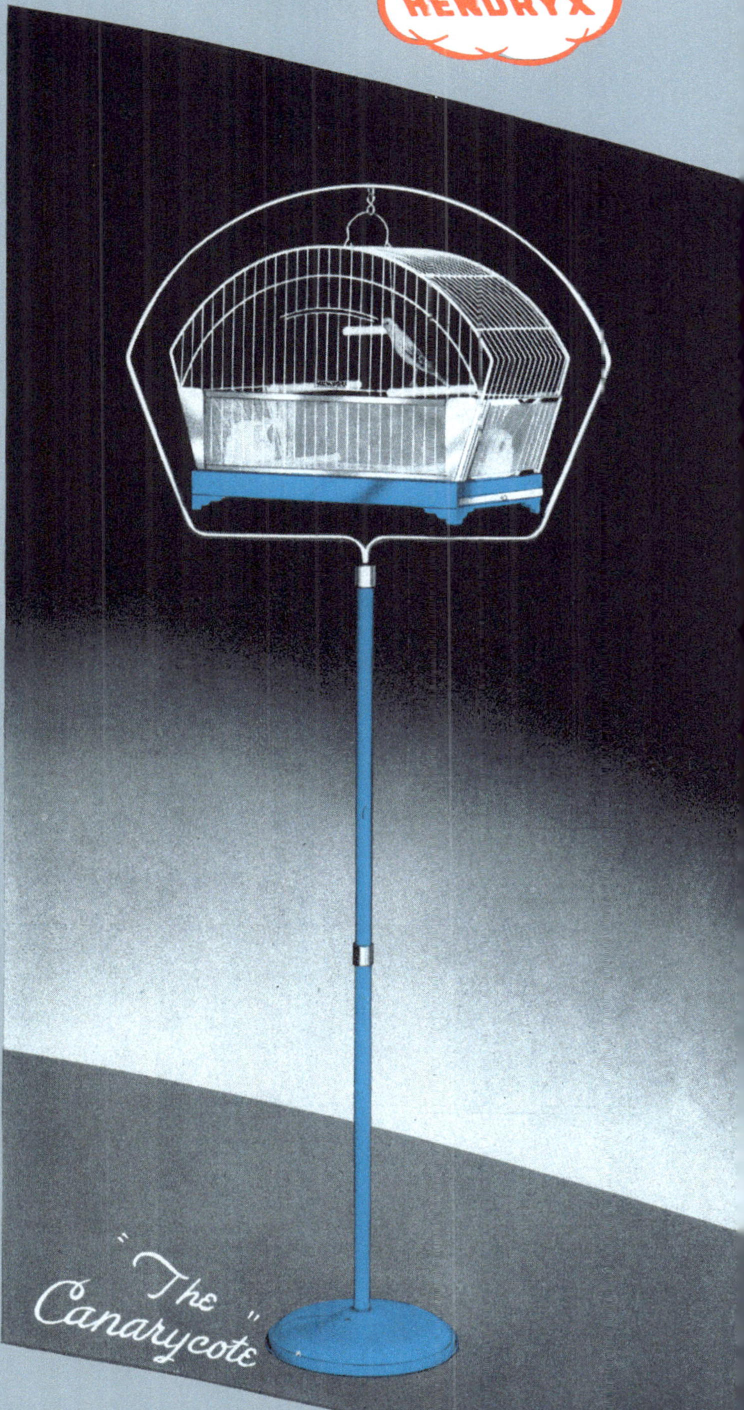

Cage 440 Stand S440

SIZE—18½ in. long, 9 in. deep, 13½ in. high.
FINISHES—Green, Ivory, White & Blue, Chromium Trim.
PACKED—1 in Carton. Weight, 11 lbs.

STAND

HEIGHT—5 ft. 4½ in. 2 Pc. Upright ⅞ in. dia. Tubing.
FINISHES—Green, Ivory, Blue with Chromium Arch.
PACKED—1 KD in Carton. Weight, 13 lbs.

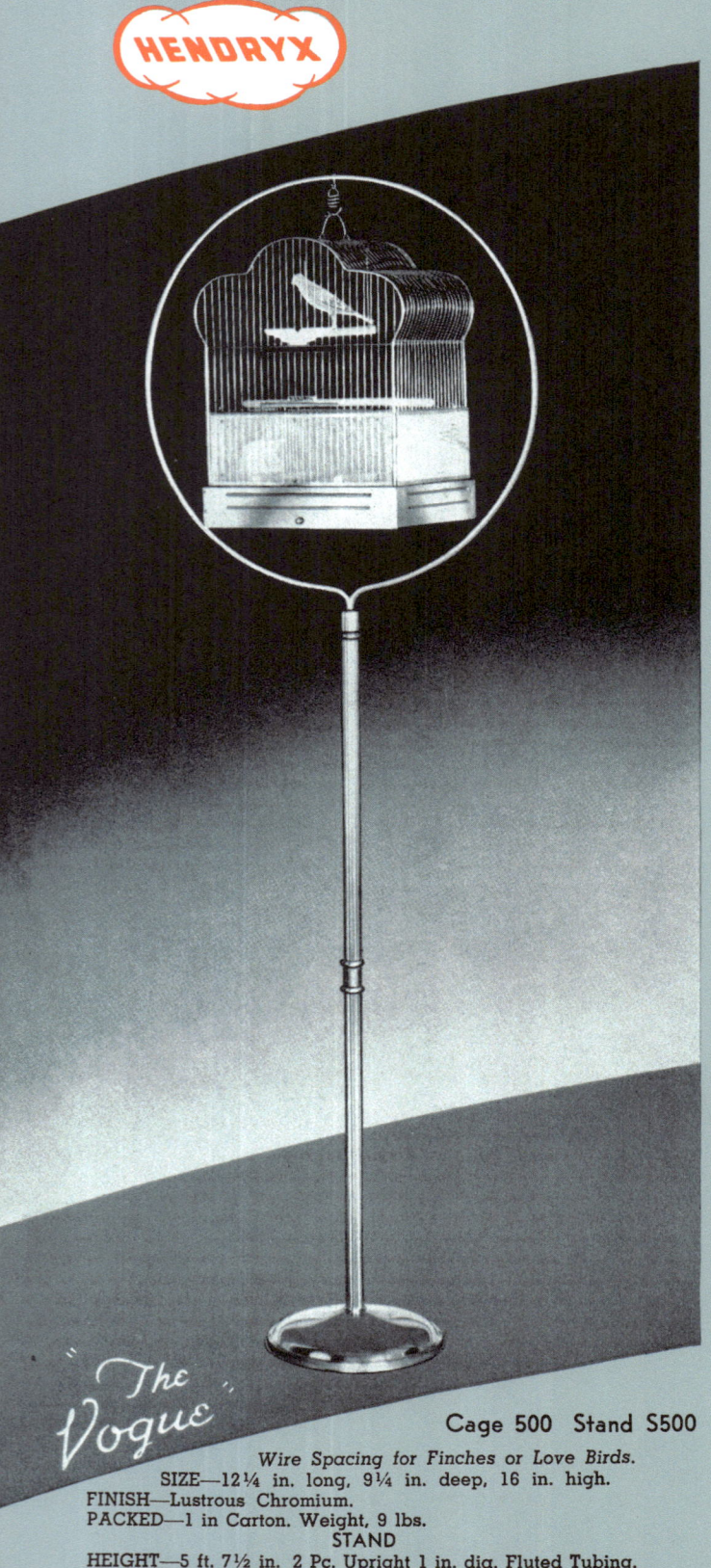

"The Vogue"

Cage 500   Stand S500

Wire Spacing for Finches or Love Birds.
SIZE—12¼ in. long, 9¼ in. deep, 16 in. high.
FINISH—Lustrous Chromium.
PACKED—1 in Carton. Weight, 9 lbs.

STAND

HEIGHT—5 ft. 7½ in. 2 Pc. Upright 1 in. dia. Fluted Tubing.
FINISH—Lustrous Chromium.
PACKED—1 KD in Carton. Weight, 11 lbs.

"The Castle"

Cage 300, Stand S300

Another striking Model with Modernistic Lines.
SIZE—12¼ in. long, 9¼ in. deep, 15 in. high.
FINISH—Lustrous Chromium.
PACKED—1 in Carton. Weight, 10 lbs.

STAND

HEIGHT—5 ft. 8 in. 2 Pc. Upright 1 in. dia. Fluted Tubing.
FINISH—Lustrous Chromium.
PACKED—1 KD in Carton. Weight, 12 lbs.

HENDRYX

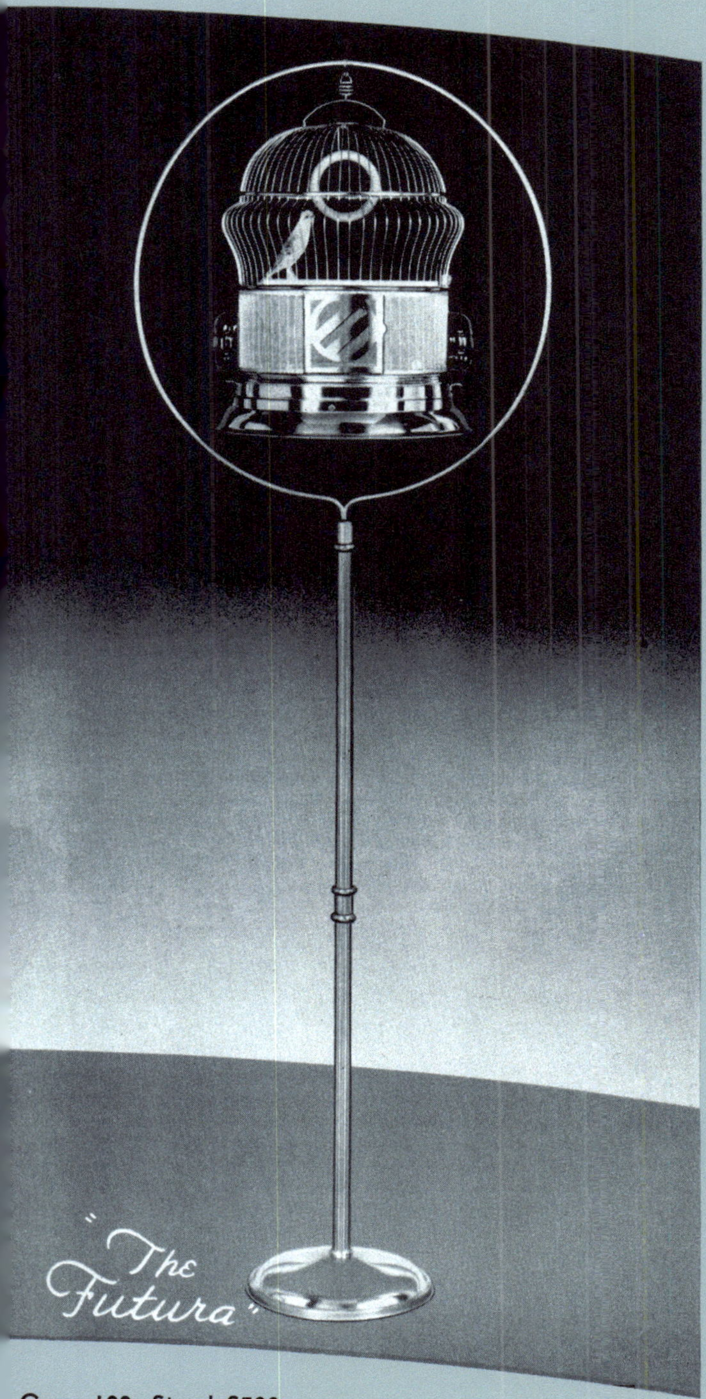

"The Futura"

Cage 100, Stand S500

New Removable Top. No Place for Mites.
SIZE—11 in. dia. 16 in. high.
FINISH—Lustrous Chromium.
The latest improvement on a Round Cage. Removable top construction. No place for Mites.
PACKED—1 in Carton. Weight, 7 lbs.

STAND
HEIGHT—5 ft. 8½ in. 2 Pc. Upright, 1 in. dia. Fluted Tubing.
FINISH—Lustrous Chromium.
PACKED—1 KD in Carton. Weight, 11 lbs.

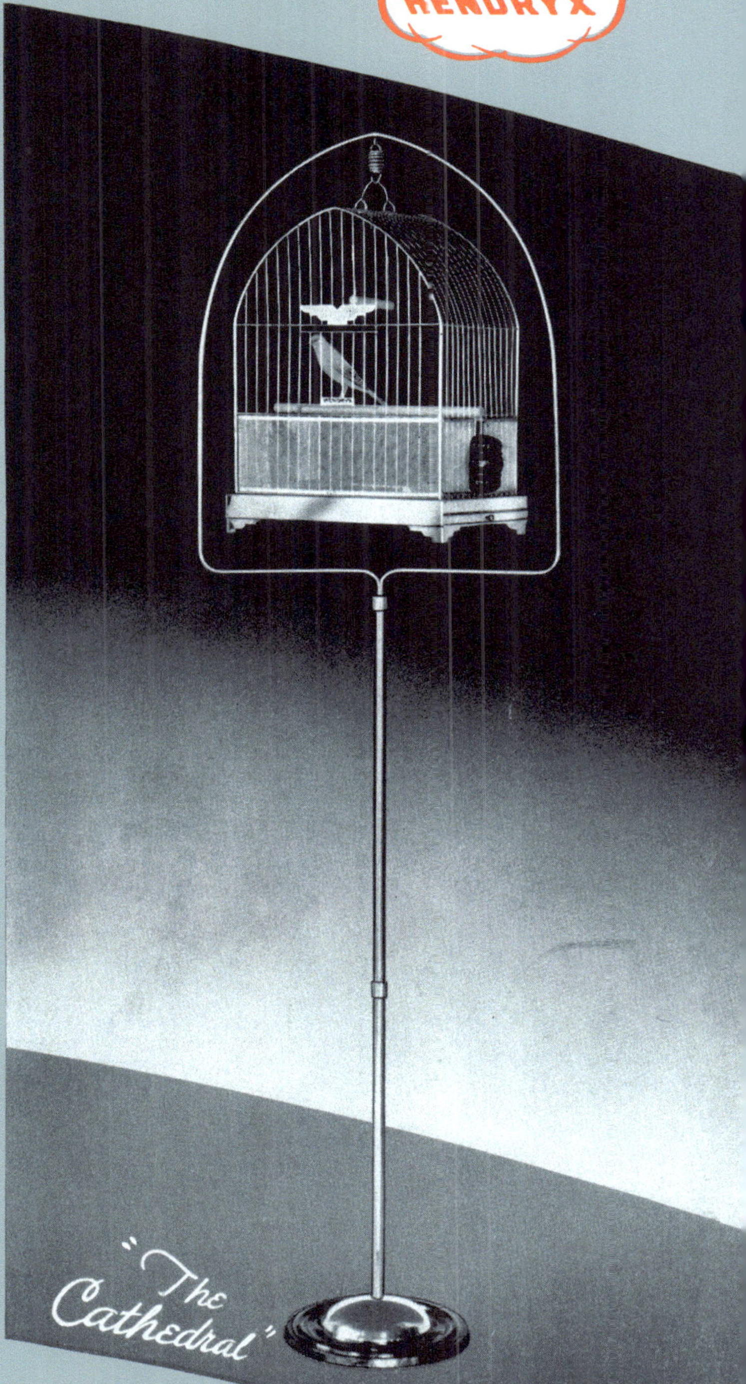

"The Cathedral"

Cage 820 Stand S220

Of Classic Gothic Lines.
SIZE—12¼ in. long, 9 in. deep, 15½ in. high.
FINISH—Lustrous Chromium.
PACKED—1 in Carton. Weight, 7 lbs.

STAND
HEIGHT—5 ft. 6½ in. 2 Pc. Upright ⅝ in. dia. Tubing. Base Cover.
FINISH—Lustrous Chromium—Black Trim on Base.
PACKED—1 KD in Carton. Weight, 9 lbs.

Page Seven

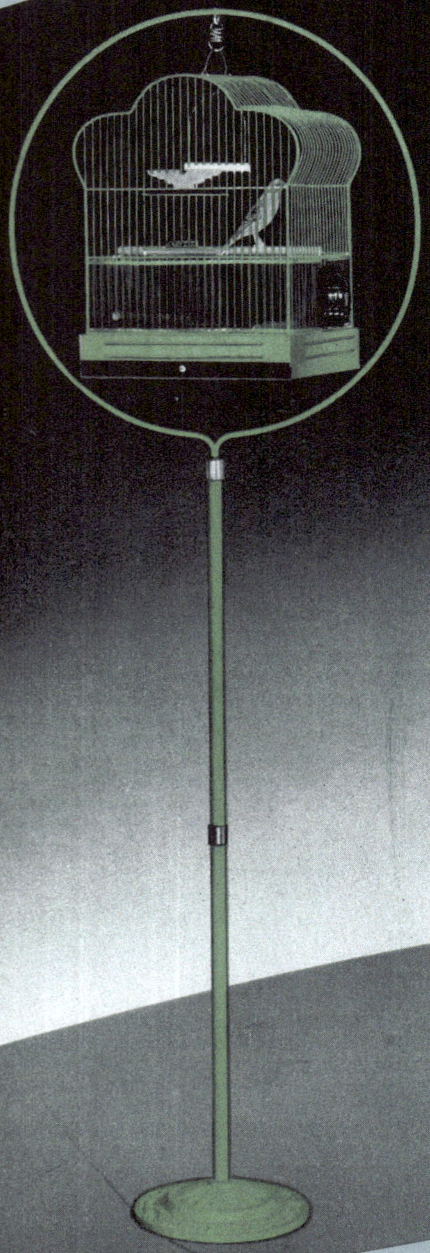

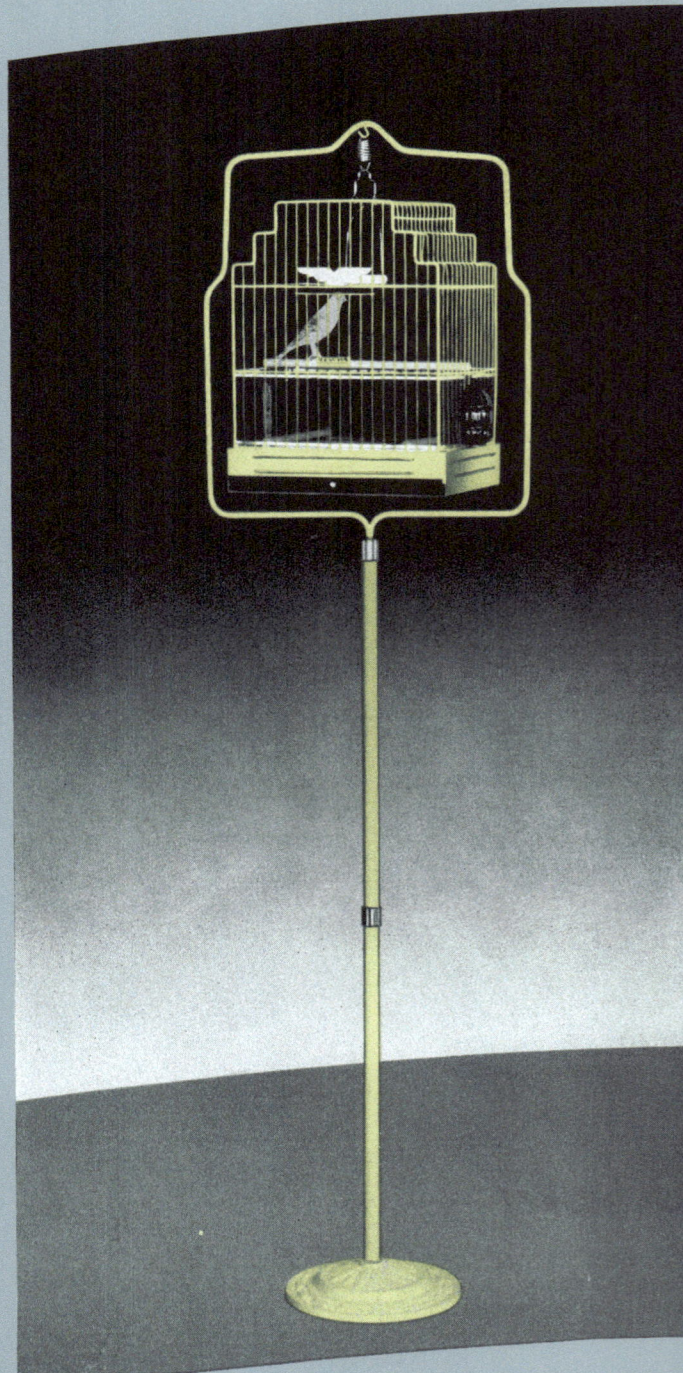

Cage X Stand SR
Wire Spacing for Finches or Love Birds

SIZE— 12¼ in. long, 9¼ in. deep, 16 in. high.
FINISHES—HENDRYX Baked Enamel. Green, Ivory, Red.
PACKED—1 in Carton. Weight, 9 lbs.

STAND
HEIGHT—5 ft. 8 in. 2 Pc. Upright ⅞ in. dia. Tubing.
FINISHES—Baked Enamel in Green, Ivory or Red.
PACKED—1 KD in Carton. Weight, 10 lbs.

Cage NC, Stand SNC

SIZE—12¼ in. long, 9¼ in. deep, 15½ in. high.
FINISHES—HENDRYX Baked Enamel, Red, Green, Ivory, White, with Mesh Guards and Cups in contrasting Black. Chromium Trim.
PACKED—1 in Carton. Weight, 7 lbs.

STAND
HEIGHT—5 ft. 8 in. 2 Pc. Upright ⅞ in. dia. Tubing.
FINISHES—Baked Enamel in Red, Green, Ivory or White to match Cages.
PACKED—1 KD in Carton. Weight, 10 lbs.

Cage C, Stand SR

*New, Open Type Removable Top Construction.
No place for Mites.*

SIZE—11 in. dia. 16 in. high.
FINISHES—HENDRYX Baked Enamel, Red, Green, Ivory, with Black Mesh Guard, Chromium Door and Rail Covers.
PACKED—1 in Carton. Weight, 7 lbs.

STAND

HEIGHT—5 ft. 8½ in. 2 Pc. Upright ⅞ in. dia. Tubing. Fancy Base Casting.
FINISHES—Red, Green and Ivory to match Cages. Chromium finish Fittings.
PACKED—1 KD in Carton. Weight, 10 lbs.

Cage J, Stand SJ

SIZE—11 in. dia. 16½ in. high.
FINISH—HENDRYX Baked Enamel, Red, Green, Ivory, Black, Ivory & Blue, Ivory & Red.
PACKED—1 in Carton. Weight, 7 lbs.

STAND

HEIGHT—5 ft. 5½ in. 2 Pc. Upright ⅞ in. dia. Tubing.
FINISHES—Red, Green, Ivory, Black.
PACKED—1 KD in Carton. Weight, 10 lbs.

Page Nine

Cage 220 Stand S220

SIZE—11 inches diameter, 16 inches high.
FINISH—Lustrous Chromium.
PACKED—3 Nested in Carton. Weight, 15 lbs. per Carton.
STAND
HEIGHT—5 ft. 6½ in. 2 Pc. Upright ⅝ in. dia. Tubing.
FINISH—Lustrous Chromium, Black Trim on Base.
PACKED—1 KD in Carton. Weight, 9 lbs. per Carton.

Cage 200, Stand SB

SIZE—11 in. dia. 16 in. high.
FINISH—Lustrous Chromium with Black or Green Base and Black Cups.
PACKED—3 Same Color Nested in Carton. Weight, 15 lbs. per Carton.
STAND
HEIGHT—5 ft. 6½ in. 2 Pc. Upright ⅝ in. dia. Tubing.
FINISH—Black or Green Upright and Base. Silver Arch.
PACKED—3 Same Color KD in Carton. Wght., 18 lbs. per Carton.

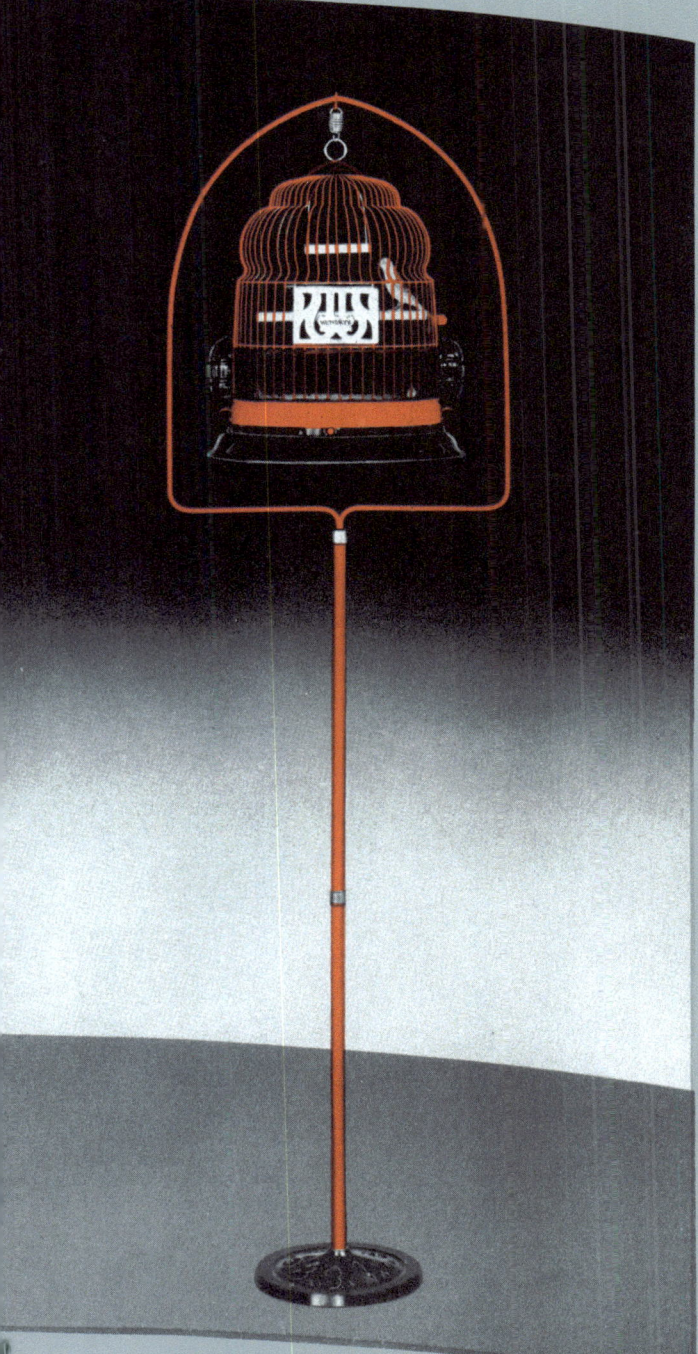

Style A.L. Shelf Cage
Packed 6 in Carton.

11 in. x 7¼ in. x 10½ in. high. Deep Drawer and Base. Sanitary Aluminized Finish. Complete with Cups, Perches and extra detachable End Shield. Packed 6 in carton. Weight, 21 lbs. per carton.

NOTE: Extra packing charge of 10c for Single Cage in carton.

Style LC (Chromium) Shelf Cage

11½ in. x 7¼ in. x 10½ in. high.
Chromium Finish. Can be cleaned in scalding water. Drawer. Deep Base. Complete with Crystal Glass Cups, Perches, and extra End Shield. Packed 3 to carton. Shipping weight, 11 lbs. per carton. Extra charge of 10c net for single packing.

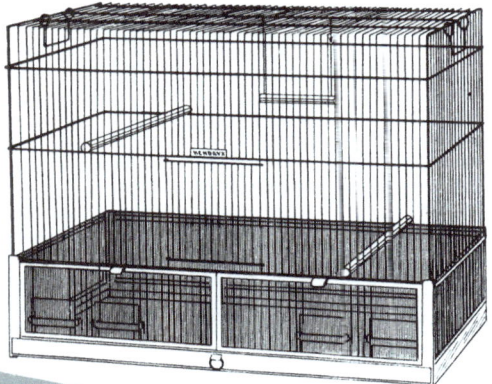

Cage B, Stand SB   Cage A (See Price List)

SIZE—11 in. dia. 16 in. high.
FINISHES—HENDRYX Hard Baked Enamel in 8 Colors—Red, Green, Ivory, Black, White & Red, White & Blue, Silver & Black, Gold & Green.
PACKED—3 Same Color Nested in Carton. Weight, 15 lbs. per Carton.

STAND
HEIGHT—5 ft. 6½ in. 2 Pc. Upright ⅝ in. dia. Tubing.
FINISHES—8 Colors to Match Cages.
PACKED—3 Same Color KD in Ctn. Wgt., 18 lbs. per Ctn.

FO 88 Flight Cage
24 in. x 14¾ in. x 18¾ in. high.
Wires closely spaced for Finches or Parrakeets. Also suitable for Canaries or large Cage Birds. Sliding Drawer. 4 Inside Cups, Perches. Mesh Seed Guard with Sliding Cup Guard Sections. Finishes, Silver or Green. Packed 1 in Carton. Weight, 22 lbs.

Style H.S. Single Breeding Cage

Packed 6 in Carton.

12 in. x 8¾ in. x 10½ in. high. Sanitary Aluminized finish. Complete with Nest, Cups and Perches. Weight, 21 lbs. per carton.

NOTE: Extra packing charge of 10c for Single Cage in carton.

Style S.B. Single Breeding Cage

Packed 3 in Carton.

16 in. x 8¾ in. x 10½ in. high. Sanitary Aluminized finish. Sliding Drawer. Solid bottom plate. Complete with nest, cups and perches. Weight 15 lbs. per carton.

NOTE: An extra packing charge of 15c will be made for single cage in carton.

Parrot Stand No. 1 With Cover

Height of Stand from base to perch 3 ft. 4 in. Removable oval cover 21½ in. long 17 in. wide 27 in. high. Adjustable oval Tray, 25 in. long, 20 in. wide, equipped with catches to hold Cover in place. Cast Aluminum Cups with Polished finish. Hard wood Perch and Swing. Chromium chain. Heavy cast iron decorated Base.

Style D.B. Double Breeding Cage

Packed 3 in Carton.

19½ in. x 10½ in. x 10½ in. high. Sanitary Aluminized finish. Sliding Drawer. Solid bottom plate. Spring door at each end. Sliding doors in front. Equipped with 2 removable solid and wire partitions. Complete with nests, cups and perches. Weight, 23 lbs. per carton.

NOTE: An extra packing charge of 15c will be made for single cage in carton.

This Outfit Supplied in 3 Finishes

STAND No. 1E, Black enameled finish, Japanned Steel Tray.
COVER No. 1T, Heavy Tinned wire.

STAND No. 1B, polished brass, everlasting Aluminum Tray.
COVER No. 1B, polished brass.

STAND No. 1C, chromium plated brass with everlasting aluminum Tray.
COVER No. 1C, chromium plated brass.

Weights—Stand, 35 lbs., Cover, 19 lbs.

NOTE: Stands or Covers may be ordered separately. See Price List for Parts

Square Style Parrot Cages

Extension Base. Zinc Drawer. Hendryx (Lindemann) construction. Grill, Perch, Swing and Cups.

No. 1922 Brass, 20 in. x 17½ in. x 24½ in. high
Weight 37 lbs.

No. 135 Tinned, 15¼ in. x 17½ in. x 22 in. high
Weight 27 lbs.

Parrot Cage

Square Style with Oval Top

Welded construction. Substantial Base with Zinc Sliding Tray and Removable Bottom Plate. Complete with Cups, Perch and Swing.

Round Style Parrot Cages

Welded Construction

Bright Finish—Zinc Base

No. 80 14½ in. dia., 21½ in. high
Weight 17 lbs.

No. 90 17½ in. dia., 25 in. high
Weight 22 lbs.

3 Sizes

No. 180 18 in. x 18 in. x 24 in. Weight Single 25 lbs.
No. 160 16 in. x 16 in. x 23 in. Weight Single 22 lbs.
No. 140 14 in. x 14 in. x 21 in. Weight Single 20 lbs.

Above cages can be nested for shipment to save freight but all 3 sizes must be included for nesting. Weight 48 lbs. nested.

Porcelain Parrot Cup

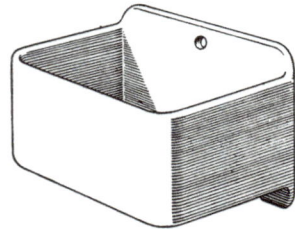

No. A Cups

White Porcelain,

Colored Porcelain, Red, Green, Black, Ivory

Crystal Glass

No. 1928 Cup
Non-breakable
Ivory, Red, Green, Black

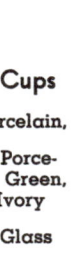

Parrot Swing

No. 1936 Cup
3¼ in. across Lugs
White Porcelain

No. 1932 Cup
2½ in. across Lugs
White Porcelain

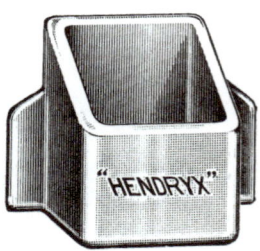

No. 1916 Cup
3⅛ in. across Lugs
Flint Glass

No. 80 Cup
2 in. dia., 1¼ in. high
Opal Glass

Food Holder
White Porcelain

Round Wood Perches for Parrot Cages
1⅛ in. dia. x Cage Length   4 ft. Lengths

Bath Dish
Opal Glass 5 in. Long

Tinned Wire Nest

No. 5 Parrot or Macaw Chain
40 in. Long Overall   ½ Doz. in Box

HENDRYX BIRD

Hendryx Bird Cage Accessories are designed for Bird Comfort and Conform to the high standard of quality built into Hendryx Cages.

No. 140 Spring
Mounted on Card
Brass
Chromium
Packed 3 Doz. in Box

No. 145 Spring
Mounted on Card
Brass—Chromium
Packed 3 Doz. in Box

No. 182 Spring
With 2 ft. Chain
Brass Finish

Round Cedar Swing
2¾ in. inside dia.

Easy Grip Cedar Swing

NEW!
Every Bird Owner wants one. Made of spring brass wire Chrome finish. Riveted to spring clip. Will not rust. Mounted 1 doz. on Display Card.

Easy Grip Perches
7½ in., 9 in., 10 in., 11 in., 12 in. Sizes
Easy Grip Perch Stock, 3 ft. Lengths

Spring Perches (9 in. Long)
Easy Grip
½" Dia. Straight Wood

Straight Swing
Tinned Hanger

Crystal Fountain
Easily attached, large capacity, a great convenience
Nickel Trough with Glass Globe
Extra Globes

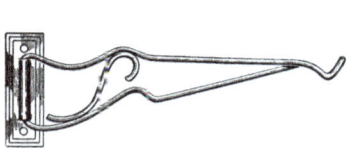

C J Hooks (10 in. Long)
Mounted on Card with Screws
Brass, Nickel, Green, Ivory
Packed 3 Doz., Assorted in box

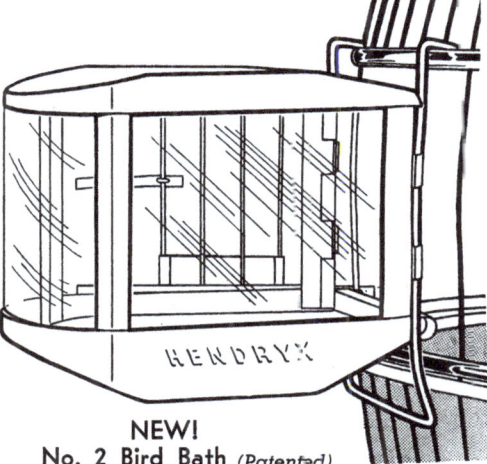

NEW!
No. 2 Bird Bath *(Patented)*
The most practical, durable Bath on the market. New adjustable wire Hook and Guard conforms to any size of Door or shape of Cage. Packed in individual cartons.
Red, Green, Black, White, Silver
Brass — Chromium

CAGE ACCESSORIES

Add to your Profits by carrying a full line of Hendryx Bird Cage Accessories.

TRADE PRICE LIST

APPLYING TO 1938 CATALOG

No. 46

EFFECTIVE OCTOBER 1, 1937

ALL PRICES F.O.B. NEW HAVEN, CONN.

These Prices Supersede All Previously Quoted Prices And Are Subject To Change Without Notice.

TERMS 2% 10 DAYS, NET 30 DAYS

EXPORT PACKING—All goods are packed in domestic paper cartons. If wooden cases are desired for export packing, add 10c additional packing charge for each cage or stand.

WE SUGGEST
The removal of this Price List from catalog, and the use of catalog in your Bird Cage Department for ready reference by your sales people.

THE ANDREW B. HENDRYX COMPANY
NEW HAVEN, CONN., U. S. A.

CAGES AND STANDS

PAGE 3

Cage 2075 .... $5.75
Stand S700 .... 3.75
                              Complete $9.50

Cage 475 .... $5.25
Stand S475 .... 3.25
                              Complete $8.50

PAGE 4

Cage 720 .... $4.25
Stand S75 .... 2.50
                              Complete $6.75

Cage 2275 .... $2.90
Stand S22 .... 1.85
                              Complete $4.75

PAGE 5

Cage JC $1.75
Stand SJC 1.50
                              Complete $3.25

Cage 440 .... $3.00
Stand S440 .... 1.95
                              Complete $4.95

PAGE 6

Cage 500 .... $3.25
Stand S500 .... 2.95
                              Complete $6.20

Cage 300 .... $4.25
Stand S300 .... 2.95
                              Complete $7.20

PAGE 7

Cage 100 .... $2.75
Stand S500 .... 2.95
                              Complete $5.70

Cage 820 .... $2.50
Stand S220 .... 1.60
                              Complete $4.10

PAGE 8

Cage X $1.35
Stand SR 1.15
                              Complete $2.50

Cage NC $1.25
Stand SNC 1.15
                              Complete $2.40

PAGE 9

Cage C $1.50
Stand SR 1.15
                              Complete $2.65

Cage J $1.35
Stand SJ 1.15
                              Complete $2.50

PAGE 10

Cage 220 .... $1.75
Stand S220 .... 1.60
                              Complete $3.35

Cage 200 .... $1.33
Stand SB .... .68
                              Complete $2.03

PAGE 11

Cage B .... $ .79
Stand SB .... .68
                              Complete $1.47

Cage A (See Note) .... $ .65
Stand SB .... .68
                              Complete $1.33

NOTE: Cage A not illustrated in catalog. Same shape as Cage B. Detachable base, NO DRAWER, or Chrome trim. Colors—Red, Green, Ivory. 3 Nested, one color, in Carton. 13 lbs.

NOTE: Cages or Stands may be ordered separately or in any combination.

PAGE 11 (Continued)
SHELF CAGES AND BREEDERS

Cage	AL	$ .70
"	LC	1.75
"	FO88	5.00

PAGE 12

Cage	HS	$ .80
"	SB	1.10
"	DB	1.60

PARROT STANDS

Stand 1E	$7.25
Cover 1T	3.75
Complete	**$11.00**
Stand 1B	$12.00
Cover 1B	5.00
Complete	**$17.00**
Stand 1C	$13.25
Cover 1C	9.00
Complete	**$22.25**

PARTS FOR PARROT STANDS

Tray—Steel, Enameled	$1.60
Tray—Aluminum	3.75
Perch—Wood (Brass Tipped)	.80
Perch—Lignum Vitae	2.65
Cup—Round for Perch	.65

PAGE 13
PARROT CAGES

1922	$14.00
135	7.25
80	3.75
90	5.00
180	5.00
160	4.50
140	4.00

PAGE 14
PARROT SUPPLIES

Square Cup (Porcelain)	$ .15
1912 Cup—Zinc	.50

PAGE 14 (Continued)

Wood Perch 1⅛ in. x Cage Length	$ .15
Wood Perch 1⅛ in. x 4 Ft.	.30
Lignum Vitae 1⅛ in. Dia. Per Ft.	1.00
Swing—Wood	.25
Swing—Lignum Vitae	1.00
No. 5 Chain (6 in box) Ea.	.40

ACCESSORIES (Page 14)

	Doz.	6 Doz.	Gross
A Cups White	$ .40	$2.20	$3.60
A Cups Colored	.50	2.70	4.80
A Cups Crystal Glass	.60		
1928 Cup	1.15		
1936 Cup—White	.90	5.00	9.00
1932 Cup—White	.75	4.20	7.80
1916 Cup—Glass	1.40		
80 Cup—Opal	.40	2.25	4.20

	Per 100	Per 1000
Food Holder	.75	6.00

	Doz.	6 Doz.	Gross
Bath Dish—Opal	.70	4.00	7.90
Wire Nest	.50	2.75	5.00

PAGE 15

140 Spring—Brass	.50	2.80	5.40
140 Spring—Chrome	.60	3.30	6.00
145 Spring—Brass	.35	1.95	3.60
145 Spring—Chrome	.40	2.25	4.20
150 Spring—Black	.30	1.50	2.80
182 Spring and Chain	.95		
Round Cedar Swing	.90	5.00	9.50
Easy Grip Cedar Swing	.35	1.95	3.60
Straight Swing	.30	1.75	3.00
Straight Perches	.24	1.25	2.25
Straight Perch Stock 48"	.60	3.50	6.75
Easy Grip Perch	.24	1.70	3.30
Cedar Perch Stock 36"	.70		
Spring Perch—Cedar	.60	3.50	6.90
Spring Perch—Straight	.35	2.00	3.90
CJ Hooks—10"	.80	4.65	9.00
No. 2 Bird Baths, Assorted Colors	2.40		
Brass	5.00		
Chromium	6.60		
Crystal Fountain	4.80		
Extra Globes	2.00		
Tidbit Holders	.65		

PAGE 16

Bird Books	Each $ .25

ADDITION TO

 "HENDRYX" BIRD CAGES
Since 1869

TRADE PRICE LIST

Applying To New Items Illustrated On Page 11B

CATALOG NO. 46

EFFECTIVE JANUARY 1, 1938

Prices F.O.B. New Haven, Conn. or Chicago, Ill.

CAGE FXM	$1.75
STAND SR	1.15
Complete	$2.90
MOUSE CAGE (6 in Carton)	$1.00
MOUSE CAGE (1 Only)	1.20
SQUIRREL CAGE (3 in Carton)	1.75
SQUIRREL CAGE (1 Only)	2.00
TRANSPARENT COVERS .... Doz.	3.90

Please attach this list to Official Price List Applying to Catalog No. 46

THE ANDREW B. HENDRYX CO., NEW HAVEN, CONN.

Chicago Warehouse: 1327 West Washington Boulevard

www.ingramcontent.com/pod-product-compliance
Lightning Source LLC
Chambersburg PA
CBHW042007150426
43194CB00003B/152